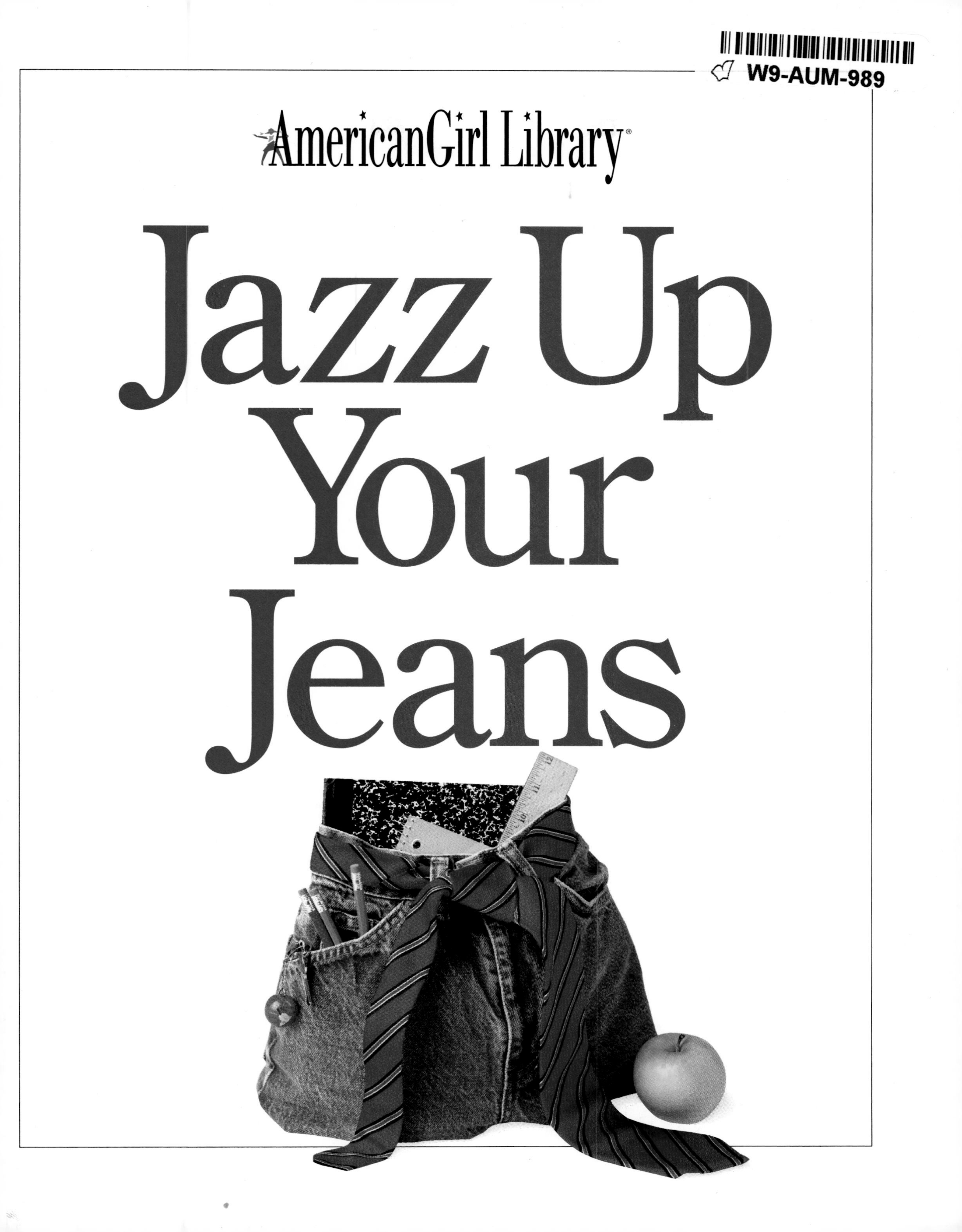
AmericanGirl Library®
Jazz Up Your Jeans

Published by Pleasant Company Publications

First Edition.
Printed in the United States of America.
96 97 98 99 WCR 10 9 8 7 6 5 4 3 2 1

Wardrobe Development and Design: Pamela Swartchild
Editorial Development: Andrea Weiss
Art Direction: Kym Abrams
Design: Kristen Perantoni
Photography: Paul Tryba, Mike Walker
Illustration: Geri Strigenz Bourget
Craft Development: June Pratt

All the instructions in this book have been tested by children and adults. Results from their testing were incorporated into this book. Nonetheless, all recommendations and suggestions are made without any guarantees on the part of Pleasant Company Publications. Because of differing tools, materials, conditions, and individual skills, the publisher disclaims liability for any injuries, losses, or other damages that may result from using the information in this book.

Library of Congress Cataloging-in-Publication Data
Whitney, Brooks.
Jazz up your jeans : tips & tricks to wake up your wardrobe / by Brooks Whitney ; illustrated by Geri Strigenz Bourget.
p. cm. — (American girl library)
Summary: Instructions for adding excitement to one's wardrobe by dyeing, embroidering, and using other assorted decorating techniques.
ISBN 1-56247-484-7
1. Girls' clothing—Juvenile literature. 2. Jeans (Clothing)—Juvenile literature. 3. Dress accessories—Juvenile literature. 4. Textile crafts—Juvenile literature. 5. Wearable art—Juvenile literature. [1. Wearable art. 2. Clothing and dress. 3. Textile craft. 4. Handicraft.] I. Bourget, Geri Strigenz, ill. II. Title. III. Series: American girl library (Middleton, Wis.)
TT562.W45 1996 746.9'2—dc20 96-7245 CIP AC

American Girl Library®

Jazz Up Your Jeans

Tips & Tricks to Wake Up Your Wardrobe

By Brooks Whitney

Contents

Create Your Own Style

Need a few ideas to get you started? Here are some great outfits and fashion fix-ups, with page numbers showing you where to turn to learn the techniques.

T-shirt trim
31

Button designs
33

Bleach rings
25

Blue-jeans bag
46

With a little imagination, you can express your own personal style from head to toe!

Cap creations
43
12
Sweatshirt swing jacket
36
Brother's old blazer
38
Pretty patches
26
Sock styles
16

Homemade earrings
45
Flower pins
42
Daring dyes
34
Easy embroidery
22
Bitty bag
48
Shoelace tricks
15

Getting Started

You'll be a pro in no time if you remember a few helpful hints.

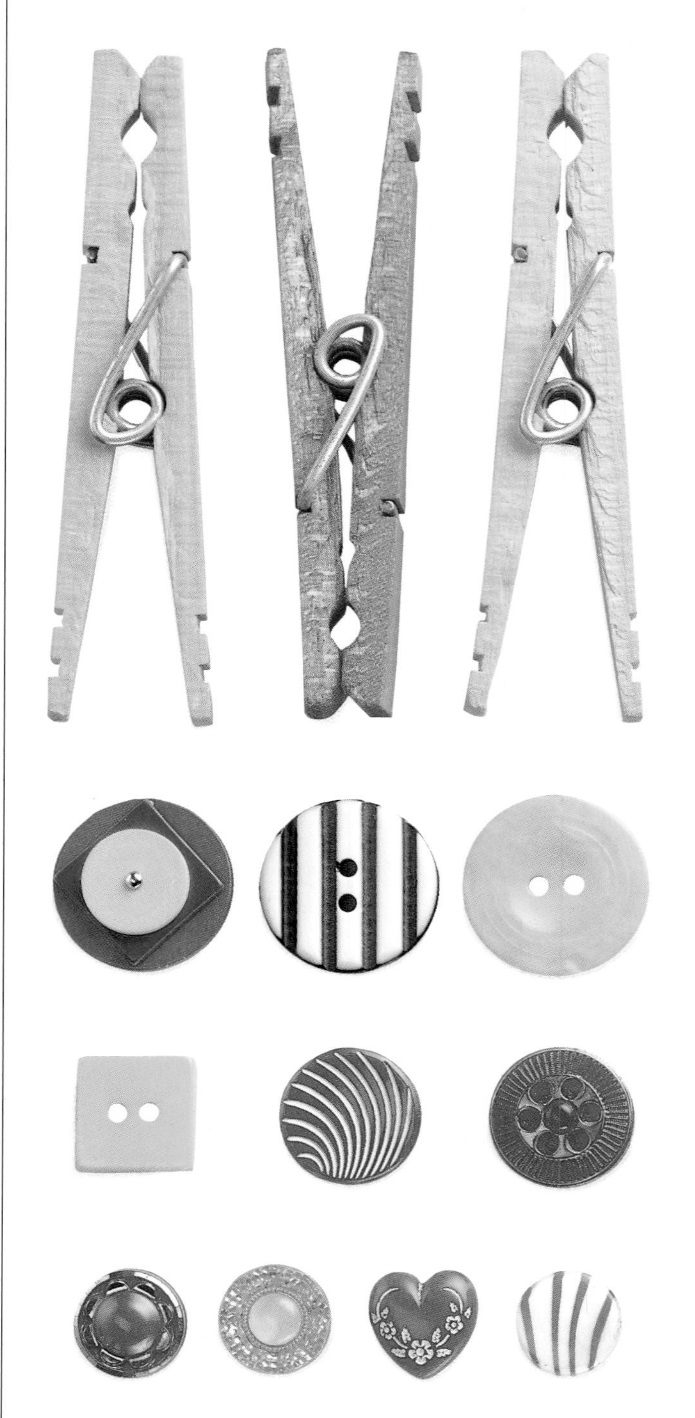

Directions

Before starting any project, carefully read all the way through the directions and the list of supplies. Make sure that you have everything you need, that you understand what to do, and that you have enough time to finish the project.

Materials

You probably have a lot of the materials you'll need right at home. If not, you may be able to substitute some materials with things you do have. Or call craft or fabric stores to see who has what you need and how much it costs. Get in the habit of saving ribbons, buttons, fabric scraps, and other useful items in a special arts-and-crafts box so you'll always have materials on hand.

Setting Up

Pick a well-lighted place that's out of reach of pets and younger children. Cover your work surface with newspaper or an old plastic tablecloth. Tie your hair back, roll up your sleeves, and wear a smock, an apron, or old clothes.

Trying It Out

Before you do anything permanent to your clothes, always practice on scrap material or paper first. Sketch your design on paper to plan how it will look. Then use chalk on the fabric to mark exactly where everything will go.

Using Iron-On Material

Iron-on material, sometimes called *fusing web,* allows you to attach fabric together without sewing. It comes in sheets or tape, in different sizes and weights, at most craft or fabric stores. Use the heavyweight kind for working with clothing. *Always* have an adult help you with the ironing.

Using Fabric Paint

Always wash, dry, and iron clothing before painting on it, even if it's brand new. After the paint has dried, cover the painted area with a cloth and iron it. This will seal the color in so it won't come out when you wash the clothing.

Bleaching and Dyeing

When working with bleach or dye, always be *extra* careful—drips and spills can leave a permanent stain! Also, use rubber gloves and keep a close eye on items while you are soaking them. If you leave them in too long, you may end up with a color you don't like.

Threading a Needle

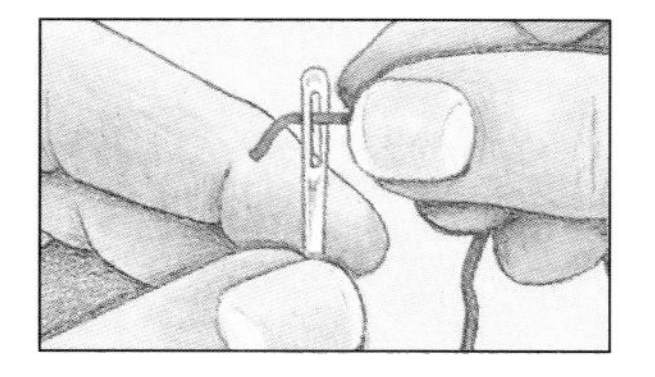

1 Lick your finger. Use it to wet the tip of the thread and the eye of the needle. (This makes the thread go straight to the eye.) Push the thread through the eye.

2 Pull about 5 inches of the thread through the needle. Then tie a double knot near the end of the longer piece.

Very Important!

This symbol means you'll need special help from an adult, usually for safety reasons. Of course, always follow your family rules when using hot appliances or sharp tools. Be sure to read carefully all instructions and warnings for materials like paints, dyes, and glues.

Feet First

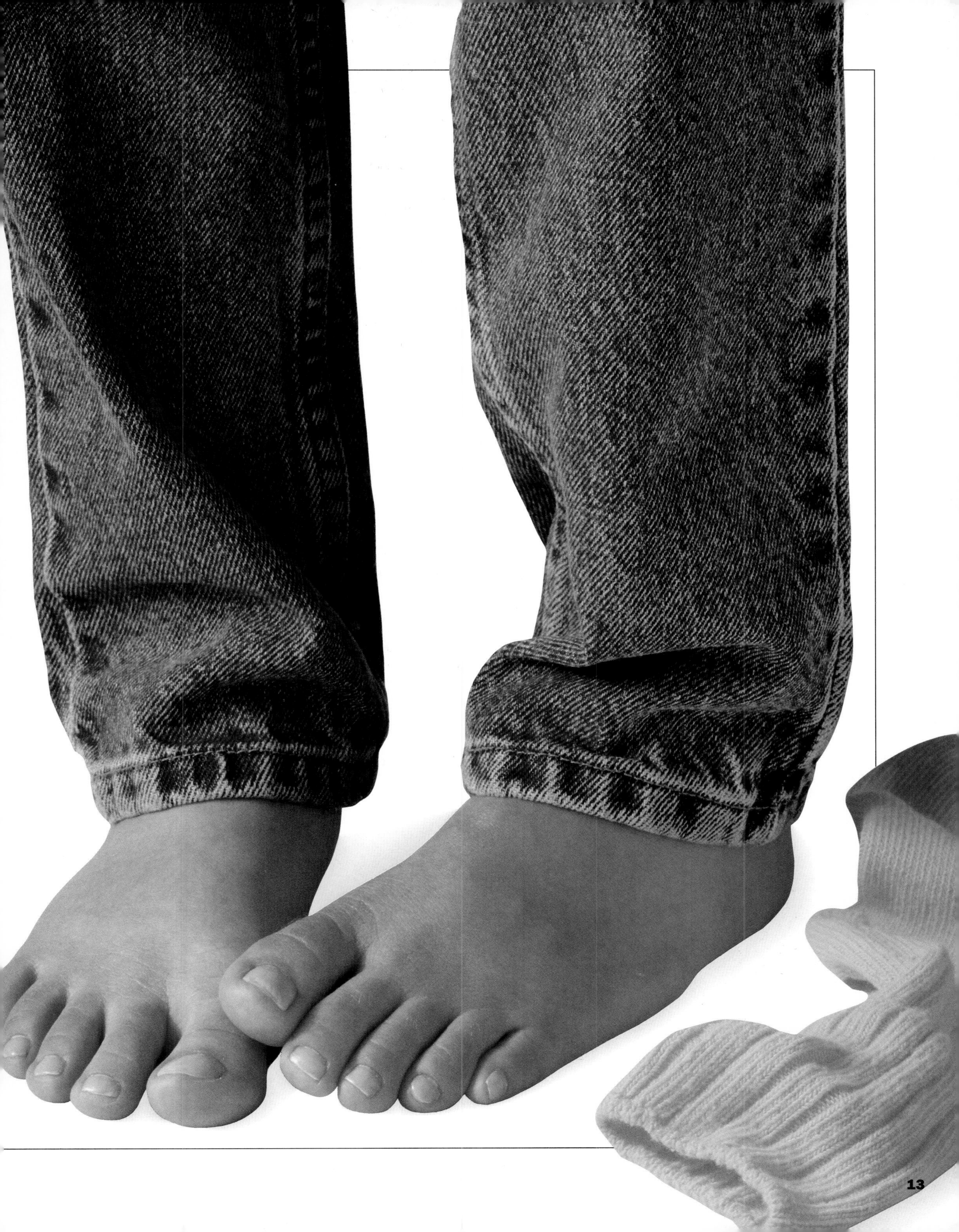

Straight Laced

1 Thread the lace tips down through each bottom hole. Adjust so one side is twice as long as the other.

2 Bring the longer lace up through the hole above it, then across and down through the opposite hole. Repeat until the shoe is laced up, except for the last hole. Count the holes on one side of your shoe. If there's an odd number, bring the lace up through the last hole. If not, leave it open.

3 Push the shorter lace up inside the shoe and out the top hole on the same side, even if the hole is already laced. Now tie your shoe!

Lace Craze

Tie this for a change! Liven up laces with polka dots, bright beads, and twisty coil knots.

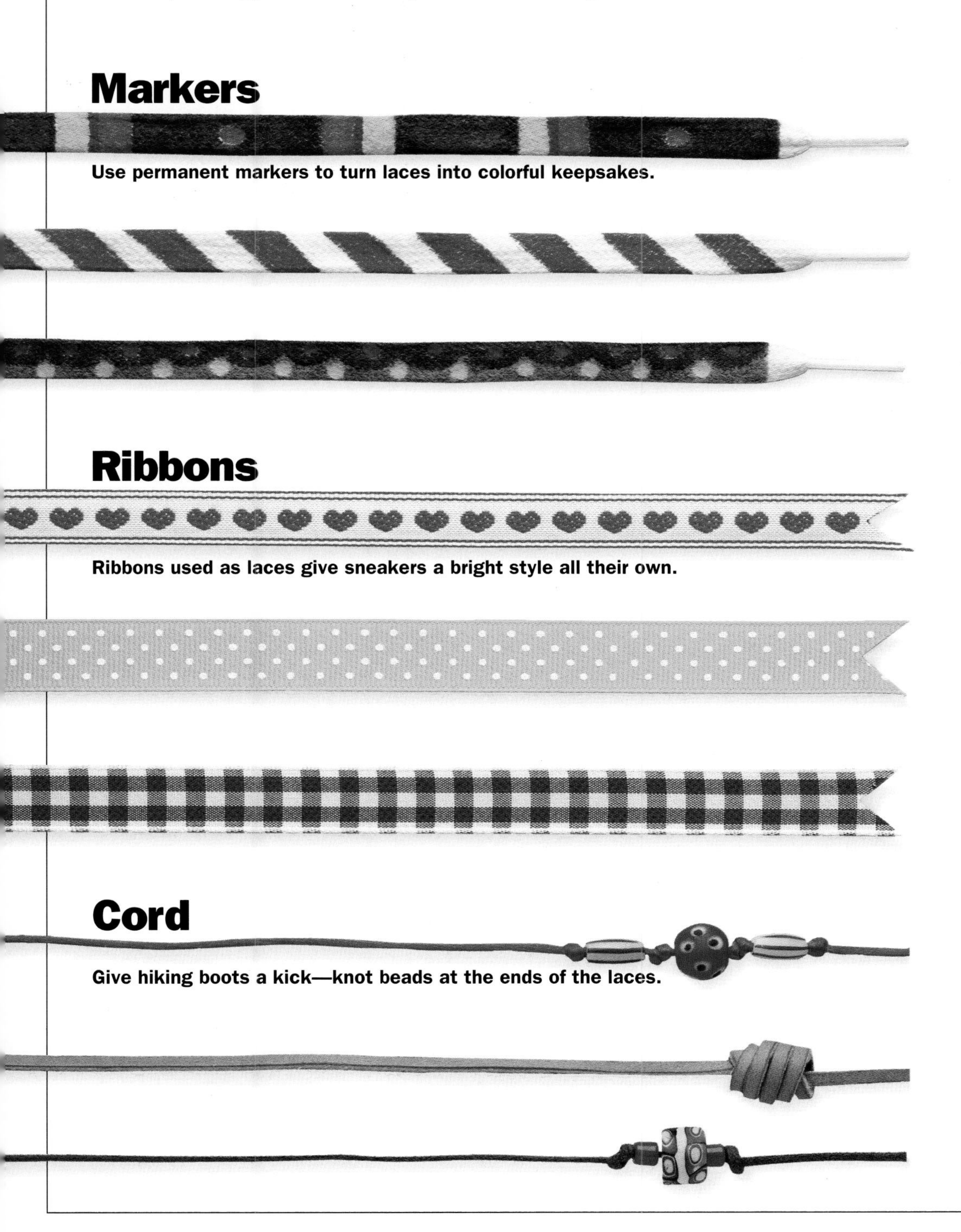

Markers

Use permanent markers to turn laces into colorful keepsakes.

Ribbons

Ribbons used as laces give sneakers a bright style all their own.

Cord

Give hiking boots a kick—knot beads at the ends of the laces.

Crazy Coils

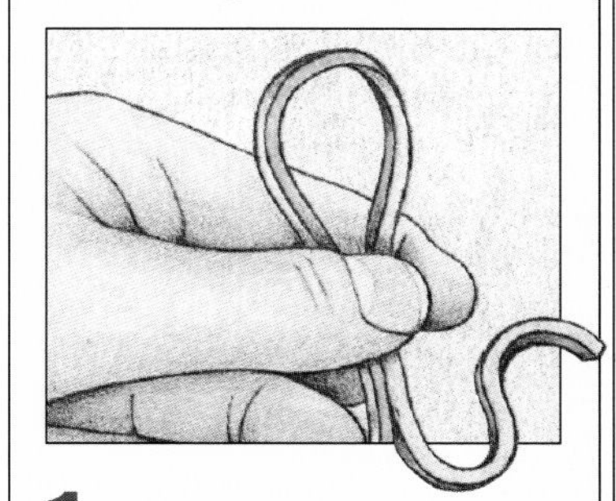

1 After your boot is laced up, fold 1 end of the lace over to make a loop with a 3-inch tail. Make it longer if you plan to add a bead at the end.

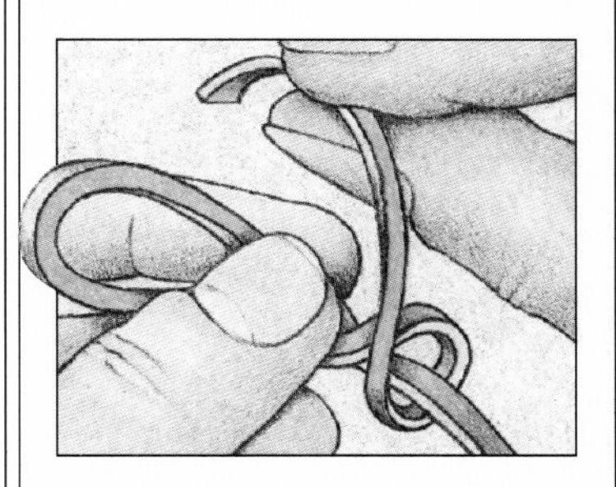

2 Pinch the loop. Tightly coil the tail around it 3 or 4 times.

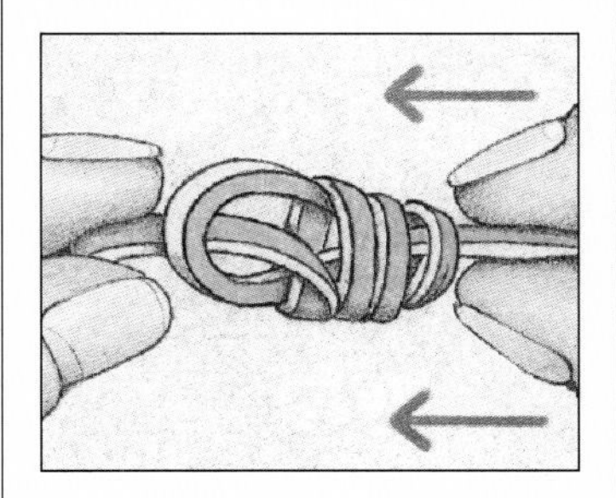

3 Tuck the end of the tail through the small loop at the top of the coil, and pull to tighten. Push down on the coil to tighten the knot.

Say It with Socks

YOU WILL NEED

Supplies
- Rickrack, buttons, and beads
- Needle and thread
- Fabric glue
- Scissors

Rickrack can be attached with fabric glue. Lines that go up and down work best—if you glue lines across the cuff, you won't be able to stretch the sock enough to get your foot into it!

Spare Pair

Family and friends will be bowled over when they see this striking set of socks!

Sock Jock

Score a goal with bouncy beads and a button ball stitched to your kicker.

Describe yourself right down to your toes—with rickrack, beads, buttons, and bows!

Go Fish

If the seaside's your scene, wade in up to your ankles and make some waves.

Petal Personality

Plant your feet on the ground and show off your green thumb. Grow a garden of rickrack roses!

Walk the Dog

You won't have a problem getting your pet pooch to heel when you're wearing these socks!

Sunny Soles

Hip Flips

YOU WILL NEED

Supplies
- Flip-flops
- Two-sided tape with peel-off backing
- Ruler
- Scissors
- Different colors of pearl cotton (a kind of thread available at craft or fabric stores)
- Large-eyed needle, such as an embroidery or tapestry needle
- Fabric or craft glue

1 Cut 4 pieces of tape, each about 2 inches long. Stick the tape along the undersides of the sandal strap. Peel the backing off the first piece only.

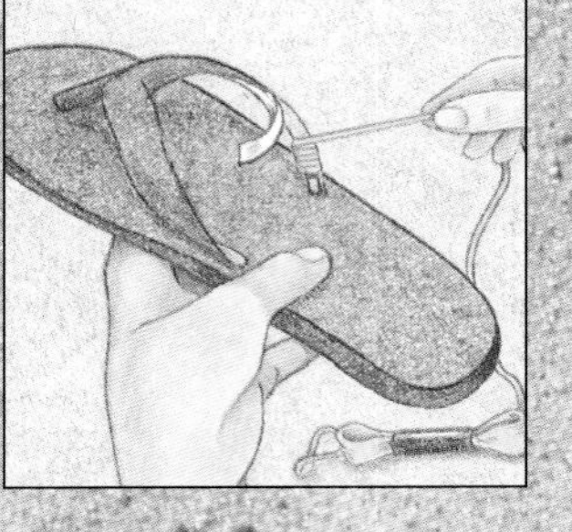

2 If the tape is wider than the strap, fold it around the edge. Press the end of the pearl cotton into the tape at the end of the strap. Wrap the thread around the strap, removing the paper as you go.

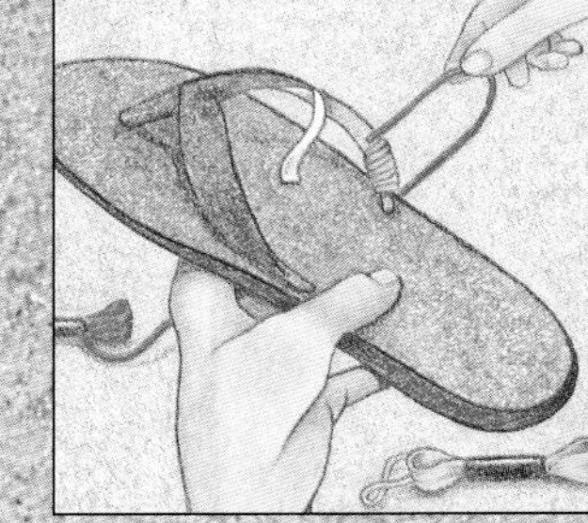

3 To change colors, cut the thread and press the tail onto the tape. Then press the beginning of the new color onto the tape and continue wrapping.

4 When the strap is completely covered, thread the end of the pearl cotton onto the needle. Pull it through several strands underneath the strap. Snip the end of the thread and glue it in place.

Your feet don't have to be a flop! Step into style with festive summer sandals and canvas slip-ons.

Rosy Toes

Use very thin wire—the kind that cuts easily with scissors—to attach silk blossoms to the flip-flops. Wrap one end of the wire tightly around the flower between the petals and plastic base. Wind the other end around the flip-flop strap. Tuck any left-over wire into the middle so it won't poke you.

Canvas Painting

You will need:

An adult to help you

Supplies

- **Canvas shoes**
- **Newspaper**
- **Masking tape**
- **Fabric paints**
- **Different-sized paintbrushes**
- **Iron**
- **Lightweight cloth**

1 **Tightly stuff the insides of the shoes with wads of newspaper. Place strips of masking tape across the shoes, leaving space in between to paint.**

2 **Paint the canvas that is showing. When dry, remove the tape. Touch up any rough edges with a small brush.**

3 **Following the directions that come with your paints, have an adult help you place a cloth over the shoes and iron to "seal" the paint.**

Jump into Jeans

Cool Threads

Brighten up even the bluest jeans with stitched silk flowers and a beaming embroidered sun.

Ribbon Flowers

YOU WILL NEED

An adult to help you

Supplies

- **2 colors of silk ribbon, 7 millimeters wide**
- **Iron**
- **Craft needle with an eye big enough for the ribbon to lie flat, and thick enough to pull the ribbon through the fabric**
- **Scissors**

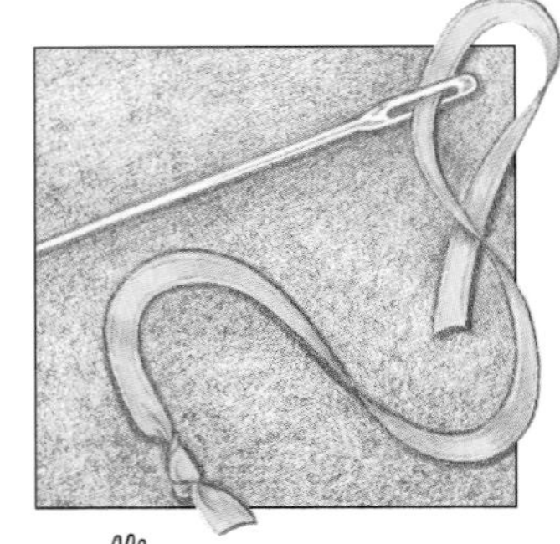

1 **Pick a ribbon for the flower's center. With an adult, iron out any wrinkles in the ribbon. Then thread it through the needle. Tie a knot in the longer end.**

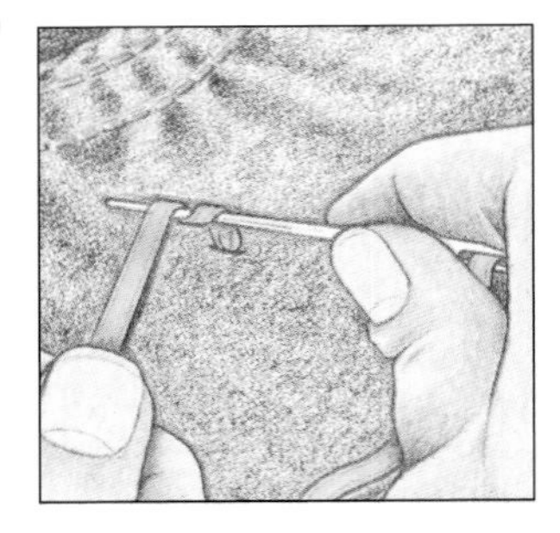

2 **To make the flower's center, bring the needle up through the fabric. Wrap the ribbon near the fabric once around the tip of the needle.**

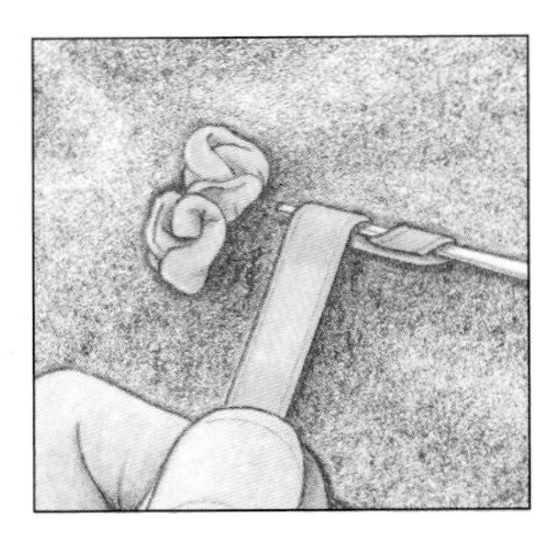

3 **Poke the needle back down through the fabric near where you came up. Pull to tighten. Repeat Steps 2 and 3 to make 3 more knots in a cluster. Then knot the ribbon on the back side and cut.**

4 **To make the petals, have an adult help you iron the other ribbon and thread the needle as in Step 1. Bring the needle up through the fabric close to the 4 knots.**

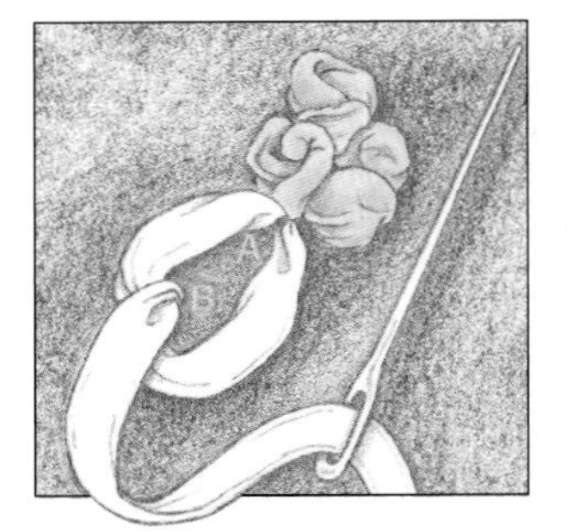

5 **Poke the needle back down at A to make a loop. Pull to adjust the size of the loop. The more you pull, the smaller your petal will be. Then push the needle back up at B, just inside the loop you made.**

6 **Come right back down at C, just over the top of the loop. Pull to stitch the petal down. Repeat Steps 4–6 to make 3 more petals. Then knot the ribbon on the back side and cut.**

Sunny Stitches

Use embroidery floss instead of ribbon to make things bloom! Draw or trace your design with fabric pen or light pencil. Then thread a tapestry or craft needle with embroidery floss, keeping the 6 thin strands of the floss together. Stitch over the lines you drew with a straight up-and-down stitch.

Homemade Fades

What do you do if the shade's too blue? Fade away, then add a pretty stamp or two!

YOU WILL NEED

- An adult to help you

Supplies

- Smock
- Rubber gloves
- 1 pint of liquid bleach
- Plastic tub
- Wooden spoon
- Laundry detergent
- Newspaper
- Paper plates
- Fabric paint—the opaque (thicker, less see-through) kind
- Sponge
- Rubber stamps, available at craft stores
- Scrap paper

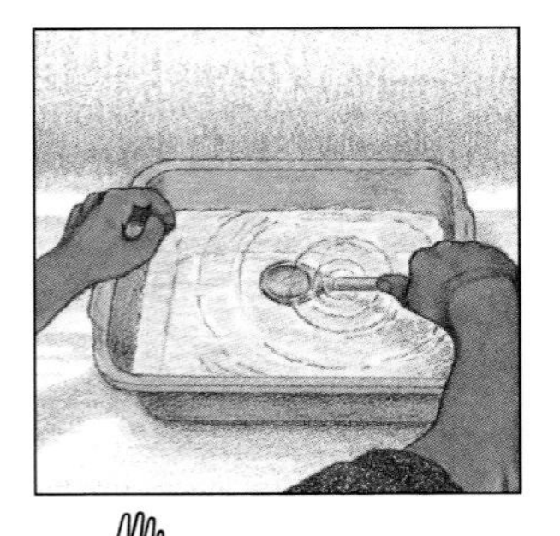

1 Put on your smock. Place the plastic tub in a bathtub or large sink. Then fill the plastic tub with cool water. Add the bleach and stir with the wooden spoon.

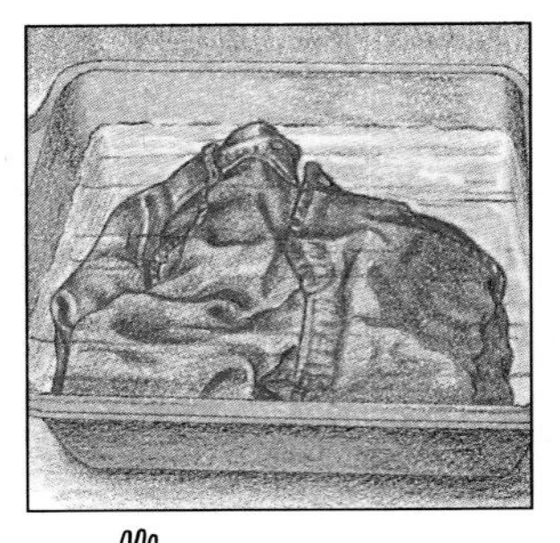

2 Sink your jeans into the bleach solution. Push down with the spoon and press out the trapped air so the jeans don't float back up. Soak for 3–6 hours, stirring occasionally.

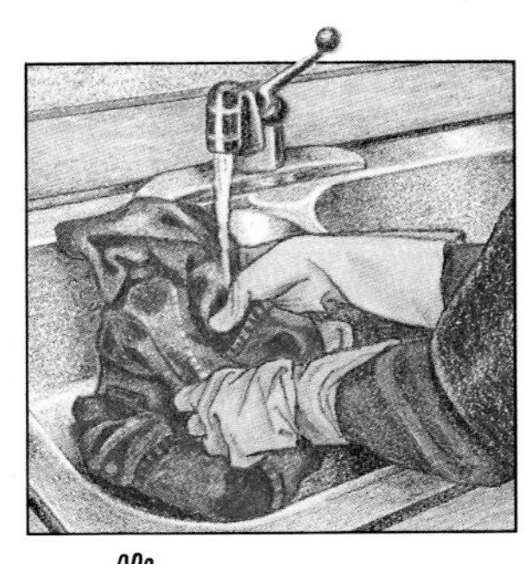

3 When the jeans have faded to a shade you like, put on the gloves and remove the pants from the bleach solution. Rinse thoroughly with cold water.

4 Wash the jeans with laundry detergent and dry them completely.

5 Cover your work space with newspaper. Pour a small amount of paint onto a paper plate, using a separate plate for each color. Spread the paint into a thin layer with a sponge.

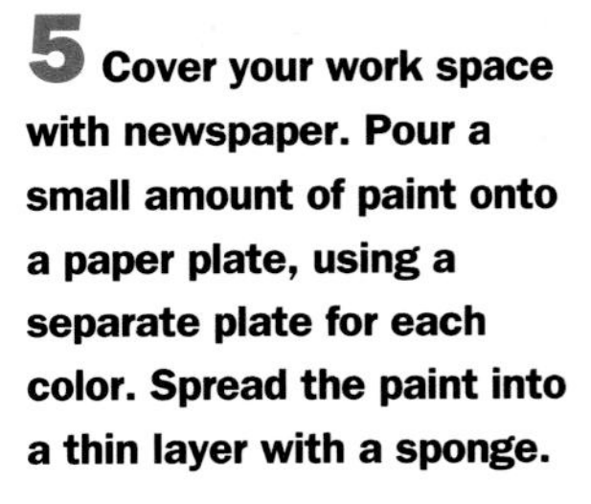

6 Practice pressing the rubber stamp into the paint and onto scrap paper. When you're ready, stamp on the jeans. Be sure to wash the stamp with warm, soapy water before you switch colors.

To stamp 2 colors at once, use a paintbrush to paint the different colors on the raised parts of the rubber stamp.

Bands of Blue

A few rubber bands are all it takes to add a colorful twist.

1 Before bleaching your jeans, bunch up little sections of material and wrap them tightly with rubber bands.

2 After bleaching and rinsing the jeans, remove the rubber bands. The areas covered by them will still be dark blue.

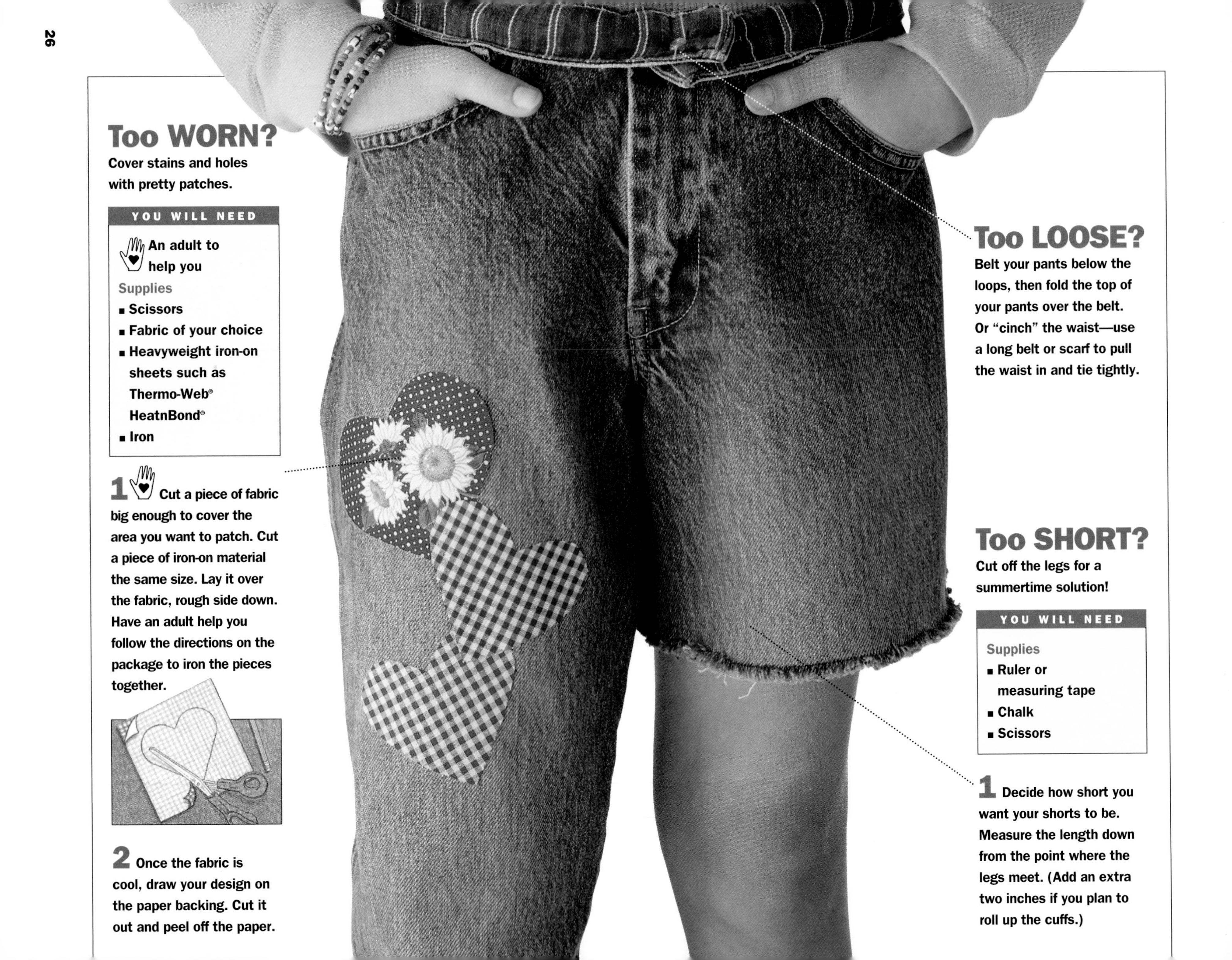

Too WORN?

Cover stains and holes with pretty patches.

YOU WILL NEED

An adult to help you

Supplies
- Scissors
- Fabric of your choice
- Heavyweight iron-on sheets such as Thermo-Web® HeatnBond®
- Iron

1 Cut a piece of fabric big enough to cover the area you want to patch. Cut a piece of iron-on material the same size. Lay it over the fabric, rough side down. Have an adult help you follow the directions on the package to iron the pieces together.

2 Once the fabric is cool, draw your design on the paper backing. Cut it out and peel off the paper.

Too LOOSE?

Belt your pants below the loops, then fold the top of your pants over the belt. Or "cinch" the waist—use a long belt or scarf to pull the waist in and tie tightly.

Too SHORT?

Cut off the legs for a summertime solution!

YOU WILL NEED

Supplies
- Ruler or measuring tape
- Chalk
- Scissors

1 Decide how short you want your shorts to be. Measure the length down from the point where the legs meet. (Add an extra two inches if you plan to roll up the cuffs.)

3 Position the patch coated side down. Have an adult help you iron it onto the jeans.

Too WIDE?

If "flared" isn't the fad, pull the extra material out to the side and then back around the leg. Then roll the cuff over twice.

2 With chalk, mark the spot you measured to on each leg. Draw a line from that spot straight across the leg.

3 Cut along the lines. When the shorts are washed, the cut edge will become fringed. Wear with the fringe showing or with the cuffs rolled up.

Magic Makeovers

Save the most hopeless jeans with these creative no-sew tricks.

Top It Off

The Basic Tee

Go from boring to beautiful with colorful stamps and stitch-ons.

Put Your Stamp on It

YOU WILL NEED

Supplies

- Newspaper and cardboard
- Paper plates
- Fabric or acrylic paint
- Stamp shapes cut out of sponges

For shapes that are too hard to cut from a sponge, use a paintbrush to paint on the sponge and then stamp on the shirt.

1 Cover your work area with newspaper. Place a piece of cardboard or some newspaper inside the shirt to keep the paint from soaking through.

2 Pour a small amount of paint onto a plate. Use a sponge to spread the paint into a thin layer.

3 Wet the sponge stamp slightly and squeeze it out. Then press it into the paint and onto the shirt. Rinse out the stamp before switching colors.

Sew Easy!

Stitch on mini rosettes, satin bows, and appliqués along collars and cuffs to dress up even the dullest T-shirt! Look for these pretty sew-ons at your local craft or fabric store.

Cute as a Button

One stitch, two stitch, three stitch, four. Sew on some style with buttons galore!

Cross Stitch

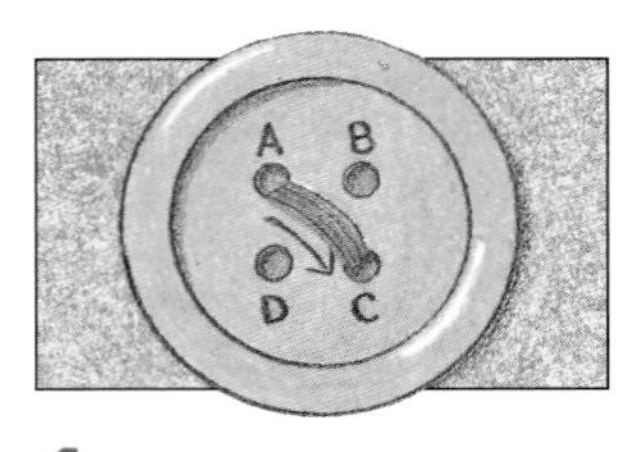

1 Come up at A and go down at C. Repeat 3 times.

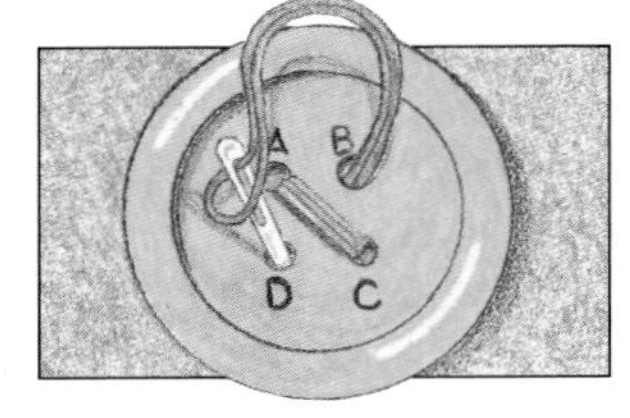

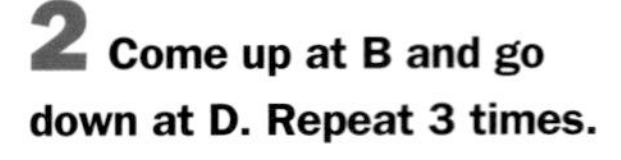

2 Come up at B and go down at D. Repeat 3 times.

3 Knot your thread on the back when finished.

Box Stitch

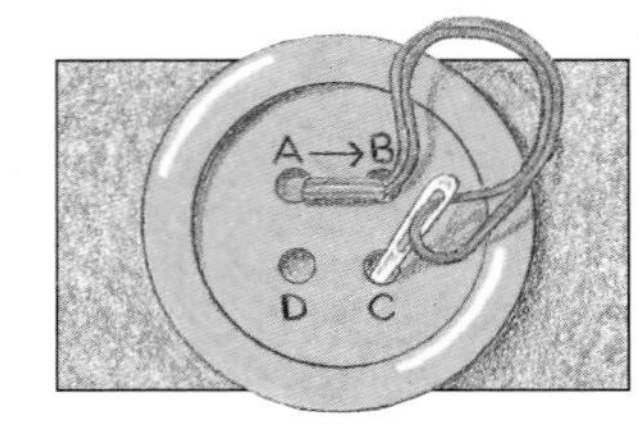

1 Come up at A and go down at B. Come back up at B and go down at C.

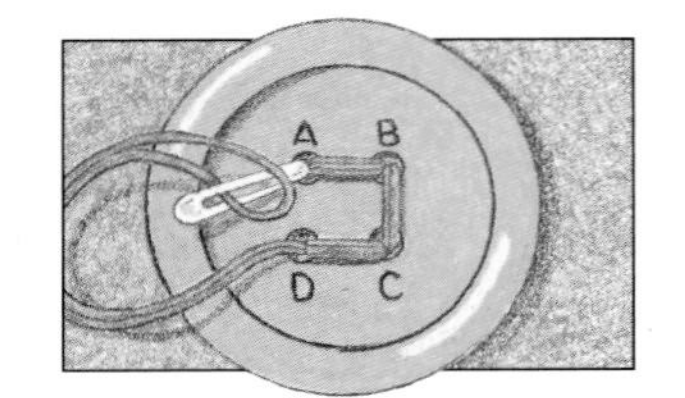

2 Come up at C and go down at D. Come back up at D and go down at A.

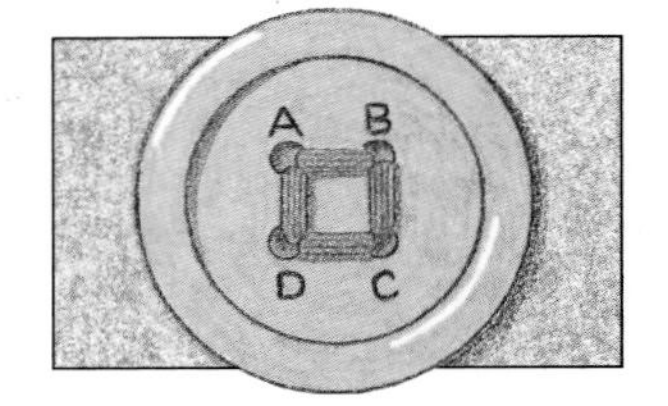

3 Repeat 3 times. Knot your thread on the back when finished.

Stem Stitch

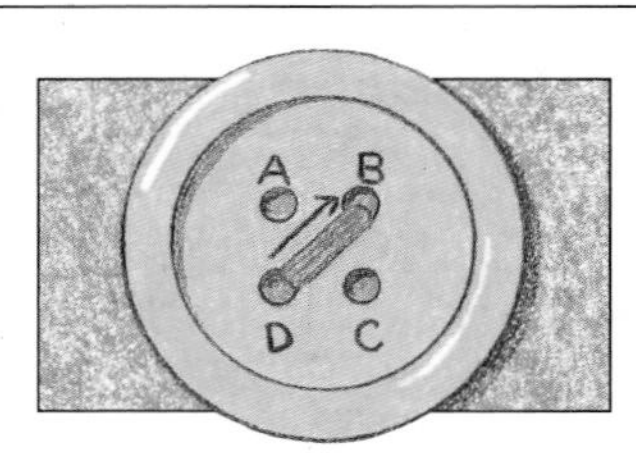

1 Come up at D and go down at B. Repeat 3 times.

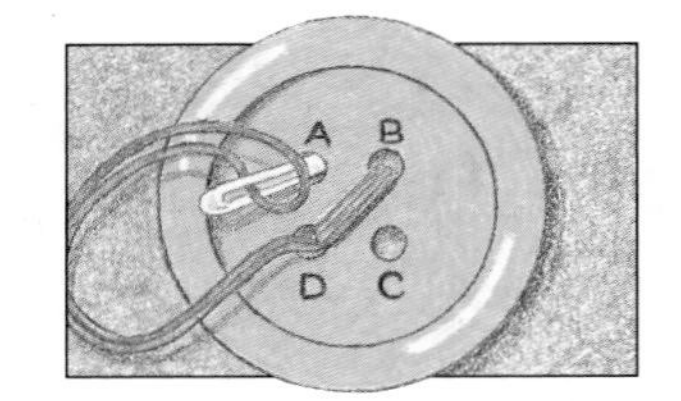

2 Come up at D and go down at A. Repeat 3 times.

3 Come up at D and go down at C. Repeat 3 times. Knot your thread on the back when finished.

Before sewing on a button, always use chalk to mark exactly where it will go.

Double the thread for strength. To do this, pull it through the eye till the ends are even. Knot them together.

Hole Truth

To sew on a 2-hole button, come up 1 hole and go down the other. Repeat 3 times. For a shank button, which has a loop instead of holes, come up through the fabric and the loop, then back down. Repeat 3 times.

Colors to Dye For

Make a splash! Create colorful squiggles, circles, and squares for the twistiest T-shirts in town.

YOU WILL NEED

- An adult to help you

Supplies

- White cotton T-shirt
- Rubber bands or clothespins
- Newspaper
- Rubber gloves
- Smock
- Plastic bucket
- Large mixing spoon
- Fabric dye, such as RIT®
- Garbage bag or large piece of plastic

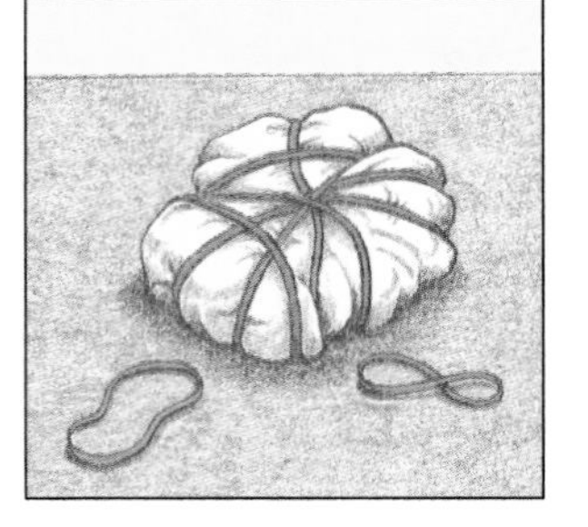

1 Decide which one of the patterns shown on the next page you'd like to create. Then wrap up your T-shirt with rubber bands or clothespins, following the directions for that pattern.

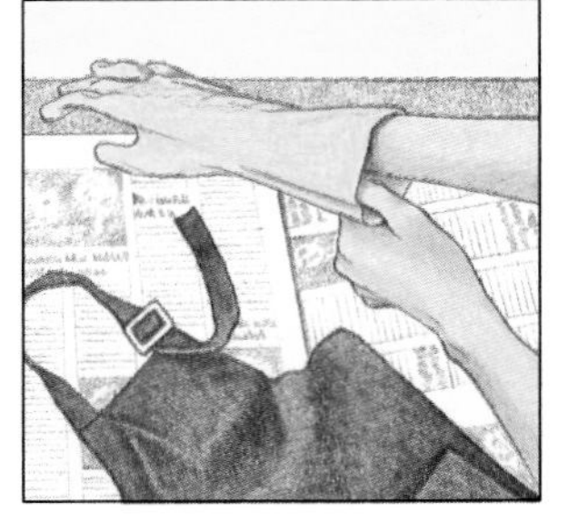

2 Cover all surfaces and floors around your work space with newspaper. (If possible, work outside.) Put on your smock and rubber gloves.

3 Have an adult help you mix the dye in the bucket. Be sure to follow the directions that come with the dye.

4 Sink the shirt into the dye until it is completely covered. Soak for the amount of time recommended in the directions that come with the dye.

5 Remove the shirt, hold it over the bucket, and squeeze out the dye. Rinse it under cold running water in a sink to wash out any remaining dye.

6 Remove the rubber bands or clothespins. Lay the shirt flat on a garbage bag or large piece of plastic to dry. When washing the shirt, be careful—some of the dye may come out the first few times, so don't wash it with other clothes.

While you're dipping, dye some socks to match!

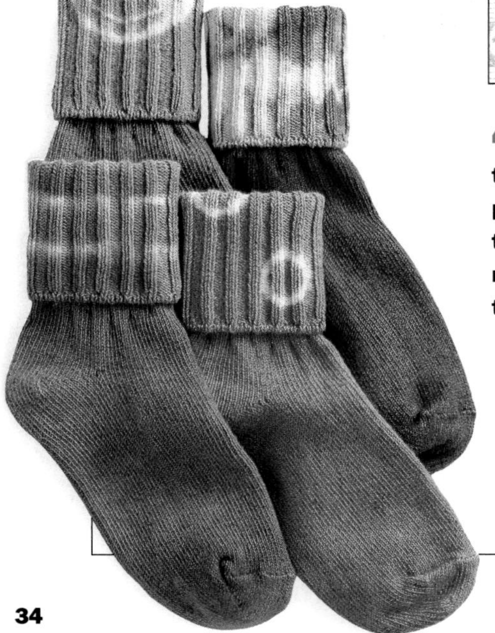

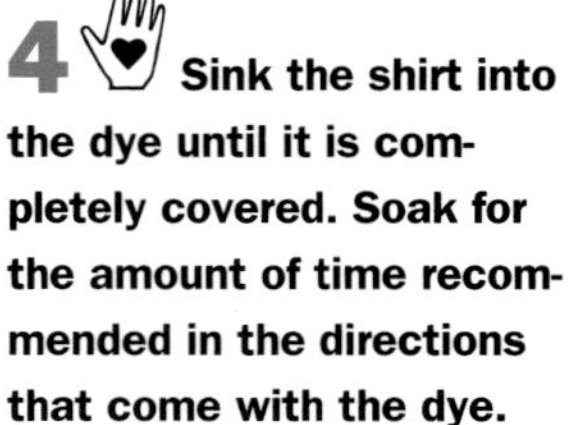

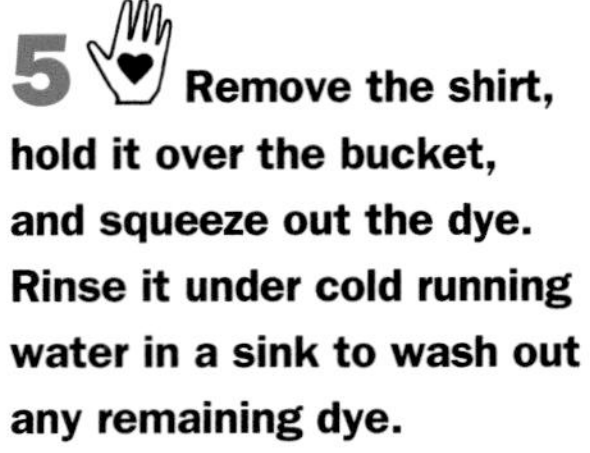

Bull's-Eye **Hold the shirt from a point in the center. Twist a rubber band around the point. Add another rubber band after it. Keep adding rubber bands to create rings.**

Splatter Pattern **Scrunch the shirt up into a ball. Wrap several rubber bands tightly around it, keeping the ball scrunched up.**

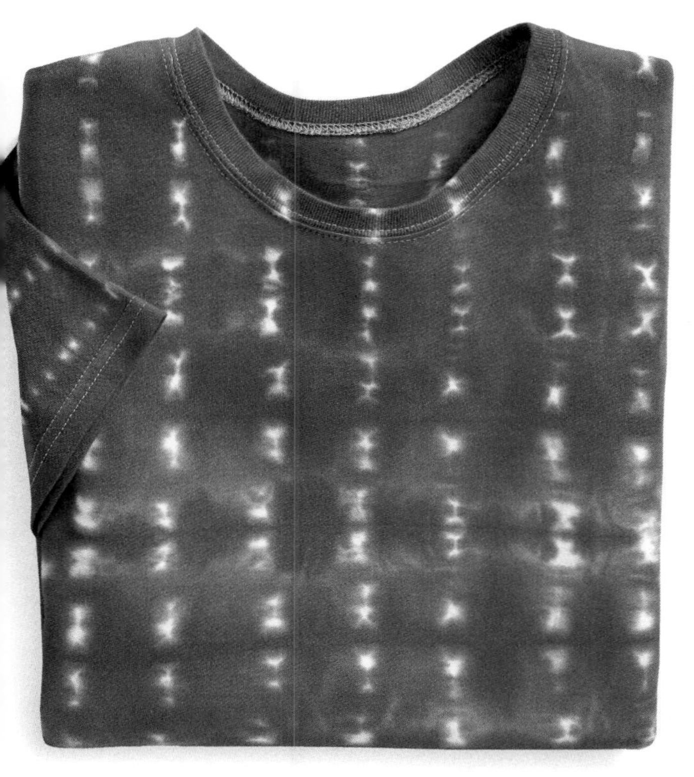

Clothespin Patches **Fold the T-shirt "accordion-style" (like a fan). Then use clothespins to hold the material tightly together.**

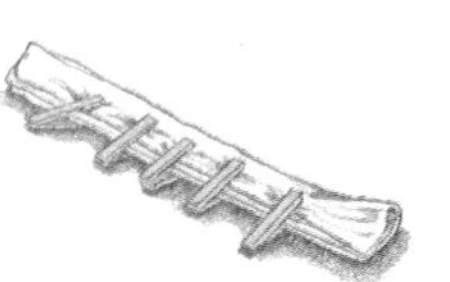

Bouncing Bubbles **Wrap up little balls, marbles, or other round objects in the fabric. Tie them off with rubber bands.**

Swing Style

Turn a simple sweatshirt into a playful swing jacket with bright ribbon trim.

YOU WILL NEED

- An adult to help you

Supplies

- Sweatshirt
- Scissors
- Chalk
- Narrow cloth ribbon, about ½ inch wide
- Ruler
- Heavyweight iron-on tape, ½ inch wide, with paper backing
- Iron
- Wider cloth ribbon, 1½ inches wide

1 Cut off the bottom band of the sweatshirt. Draw a line straight up the front with chalk and cut along the line to make an opening. Then cut a piece of the narrow ribbon and a piece of iron-on tape long enough to wrap around the bottom of the sweatshirt.

2 Place the tape, rough side down, on top of the ribbon. With an adult, iron the tape onto the ribbon. When cool, remove the paper backing. Then iron the ribbon along the bottom of the sweatshirt. Trim off the uneven edge of fabric with scissors.

3 Cut 2 pieces of wide ribbon and 4 pieces of iron-on tape at least 1 inch longer than the front opening. Place a piece of iron-on tape, rough side down, along one edge of one of the ribbons. Iron the tape onto the ribbon. When cool, remove the paper backing.

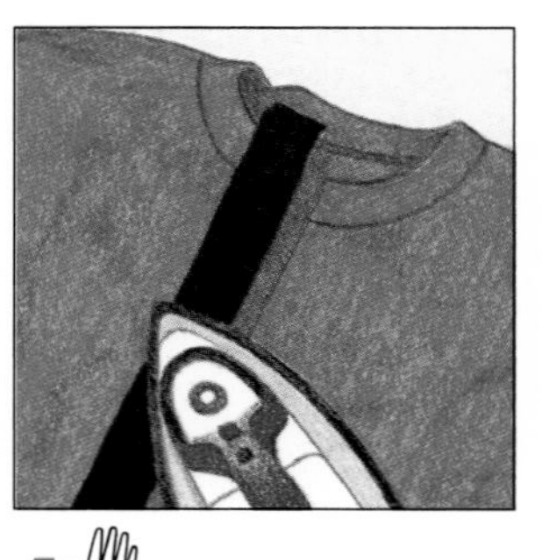

4 Place the sticky side of the ribbon along one edge of the front opening so that half the ribbon can be folded around the edge. The ends should hang out about ½ inch over the top and bottom. Iron the ribbon onto the fabric.

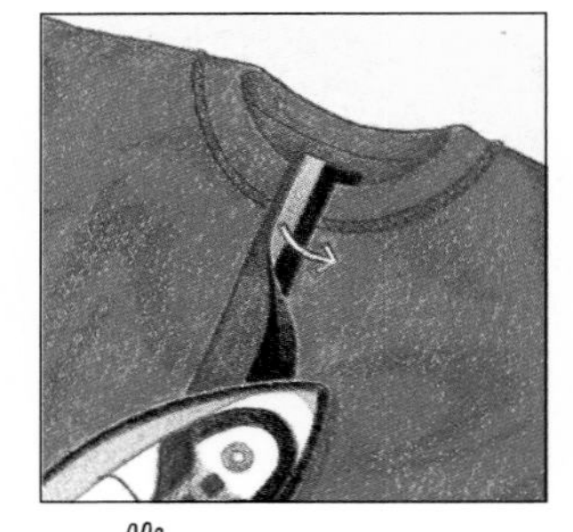

5 Turn the sweatshirt inside out. Place another piece of tape, rough side down, along the outer edge of the ribbon. Iron on the tape. When cool, remove the backing. Fold the ribbon over the fabric and iron it in place.

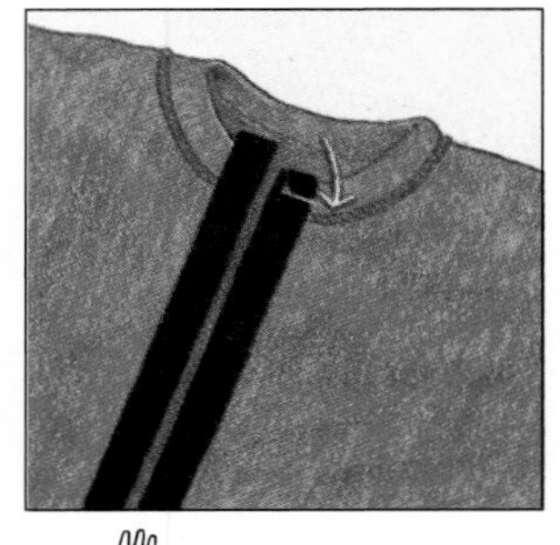

6 Fold over the extra ½ inch of ribbon at the top and bottom. Tack it down with a bit of iron-on tape. Repeat Steps 3–5 to cover the other edge of the jacket's opening. Then trim the sides with narrow ribbon, ironing as in Step 2.

This sporty sweater substitute is easy to wash and comfortable to wear—for school or play, any day!

Jacket Pizzazz

Suit Up!

Does your brother have a blazer he's ready to toss? Rescue it from the reject pile—it's got plenty of possibilities for *you!*

Snip off the tip of a colorful tie, and you've got an instant pocket peeker!

Need a long-sleeve solution? Roll up the cuffs to reveal the lining.

Replace boring old buttons with sassier, classier ones! Match the size of the old buttons so they're not too big or too little for the buttonholes.

Add an extra layer of style with these tune-up tips for old jackets.

Beaded Blooms

YOU WILL NEED

Supplies
- Chalk
- Needle and thread
- Tiny "seed" beads
- Scissors

1 Use chalk to sketch your flower onto the fabric. Thread your needle and knot the long end.

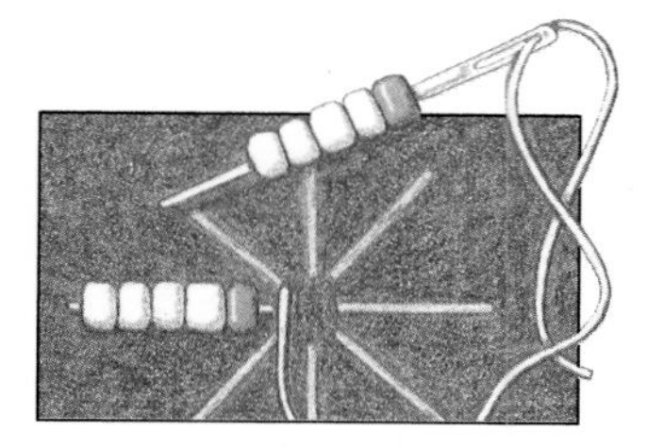

2 Bring the needle up through the fabric in the center at the start of a petal. Thread 1 orange bead, then 4 white beads. Hold them against the fabric in a straight line and go back down. Repeat for each petal.

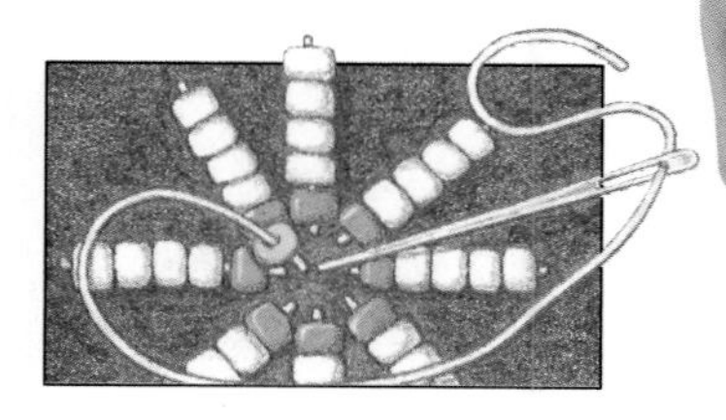

3 Bring the needle up through the exact center of the flower. Thread 1 yellow bead and go back down through the fabric. Knot the thread and cut it.

Draw flower stems and leaves with chalk. Then stitch green beads along the lines, threading 4 beads at a time.

The Finishing Touch

Hat Days

Petal Pin

YOU WILL NEED

Supplies
- Silk flowers
- Fabric glue
- Wooden clothespin with metal spring
- Straight-pin jewelry backing, available at craft stores

1 Pull the blossoms and leaves off their stems. Glue together some of the larger leaves to make a base. Then glue the blossoms and smaller leaves to the base. Let dry.

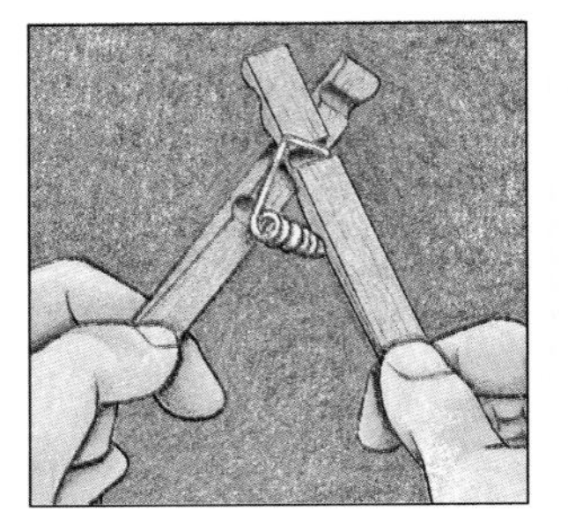

2 Separate the clothespin into 2 pieces by twisting the pin apart. Remove the metal spring.

3 Glue the flower arrangement to the grooved side of one of the clothespin pieces. When dry, glue the jewelry pin to the back.

Say "hats off" to hats! Baseball caps and straw hats will blossom with silk flowers, buttons, and appliqués.

Create a design that's uniquely you. Look for fun iron-on or sew-on appliqués and unusual buttons at craft stores.

Jewelry Jamboree

Fancy, funky, sporty, or sweet! Create dazzling designs with beads, charms, and a few basic supplies.

Working with Wire

With an adult's help and a little practice, you'll be snipping and twisting in a snap! Look for these supplies at craft stores.

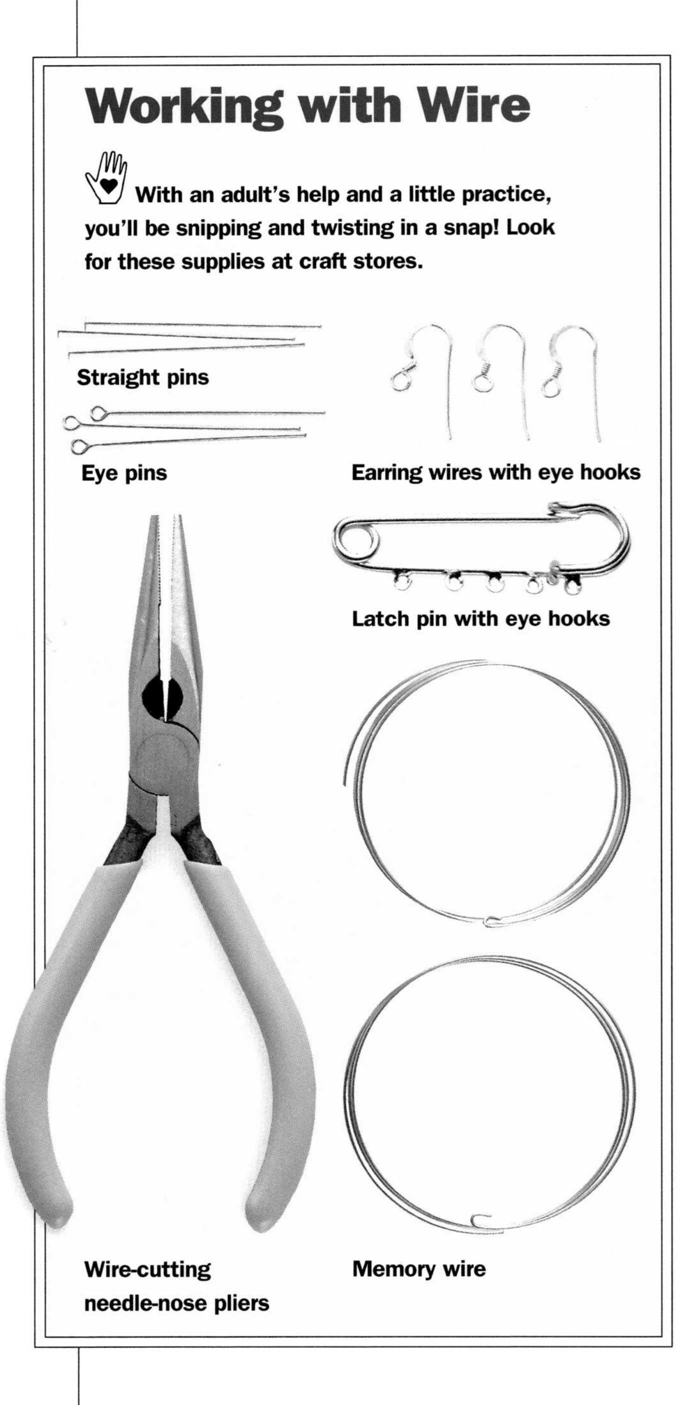

Bracelets

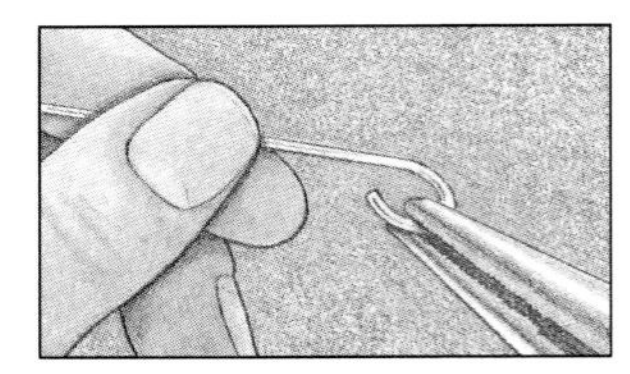

1 Use wire cutters to cut a piece of memory wire long enough to coil around your wrist at least once. With the pliers, bend one end into a closed loop.

2 String beads onto the wire from the other end. When the coil is completely full, use the pliers to bend the end into a closed loop. Tuck in any sharp ends that could poke you.

Earrings

1 Thread several beads onto a straight pin. With wire cutters, snip off the part of the pin left after the last bead, leaving about ¼ inch at the end.

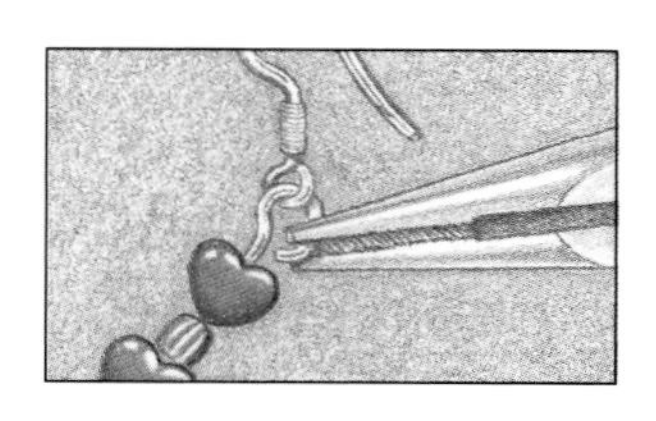

2 Use pliers to bend the end into a tiny hook. Hook it through the eye of the earring wire and use the pliers to squeeze the hook closed.

Necklaces

Use leather *tigertail* cord to make bead necklaces. Tie knots before and after the beads to keep them in place.

Pins

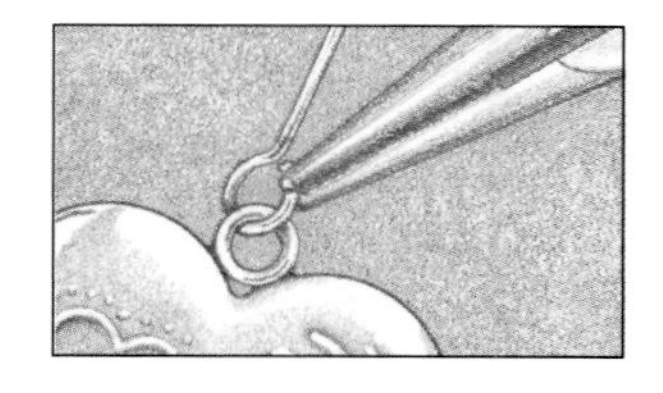

1 Use straight pins or eye pins for the dangling parts. With an eye pin, you can use pliers to open the eye at the end, slip on a charm, then close back up.

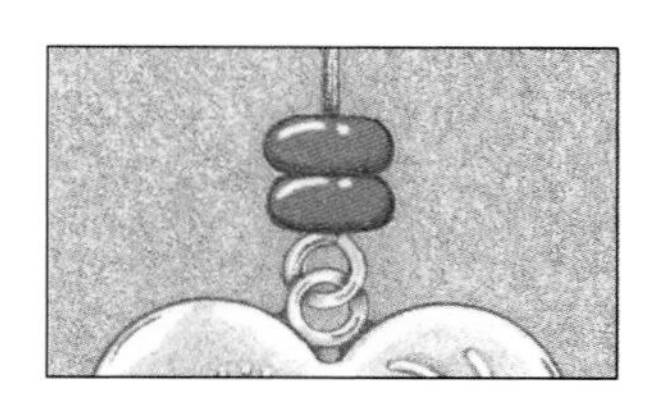

2 Thread beads onto the straight part of either the eye pin or straight pin. Use more beads for a longer dangling piece, fewer beads for a shorter one.

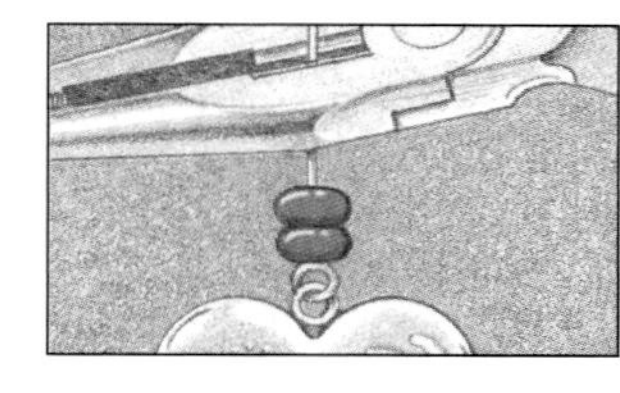

3 With wire cutters, snip off the part of the pin left after the last bead, leaving a bit at the end. Use pliers to bend it into a tiny hook.

4 Hook the end through an eye on the latch pin. Squeeze the hook closed with pliers. Repeat Steps 1–4 for each of the eyes.

Bottoms Up!

Don't despair if your favorite pair is all washed up—
Make this simple denim sack and bag those blues.

YOU WILL NEED

An adult to help you

Supplies

- **Hopeless jeans**
- **Measuring tape or ruler**
- **Pins**
- **Scissors**
- **Heavyweight iron-on tape such as Wonder-Under® or Thermo-Web® HeatnBond®**
- **Iron**
- **Rope or cord**

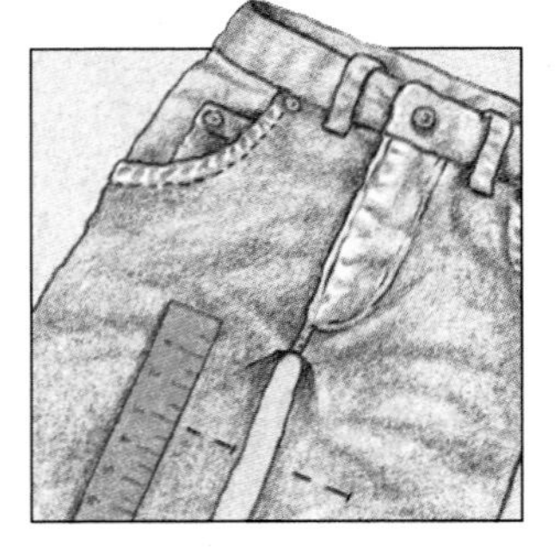

1 **Lay the pants flat. From where the legs come together, measure 3 inches down and mark the spot with a pin on each pant leg.**

2 **Starting at the pin, cut straight across each leg. Discard the bottom pieces.**

3 **Cut a piece of iron-on tape the width of each leg hole. Following the directions on the package, iron the tape along the bottom edge of each pant leg.**

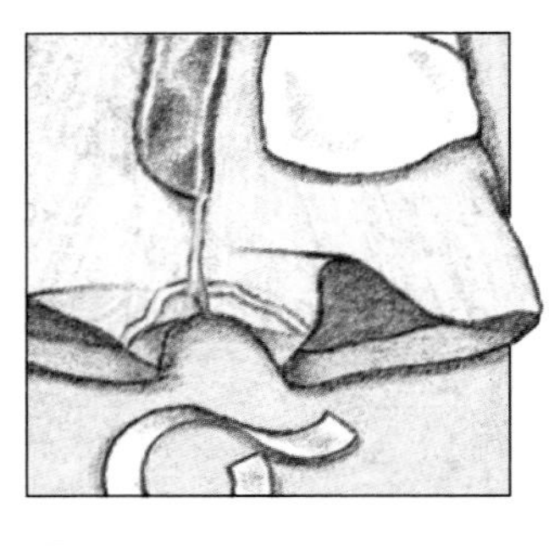

4 **When the tape is cool, remove the paper backing. Turn the pants inside out.**

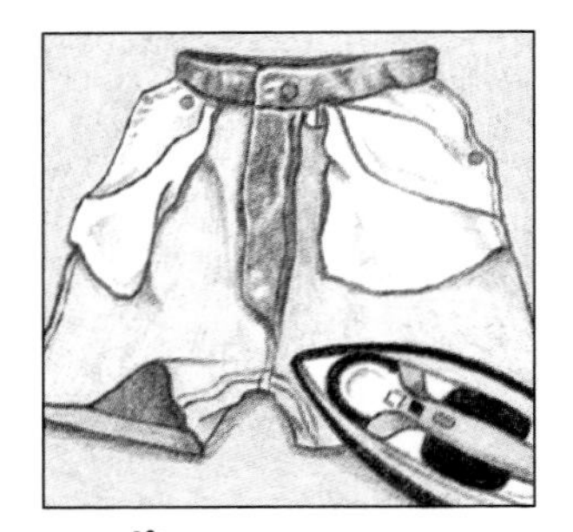

5 **To seal the bottom edges of the legs together, press with a hot iron. When cool, turn right side out.**

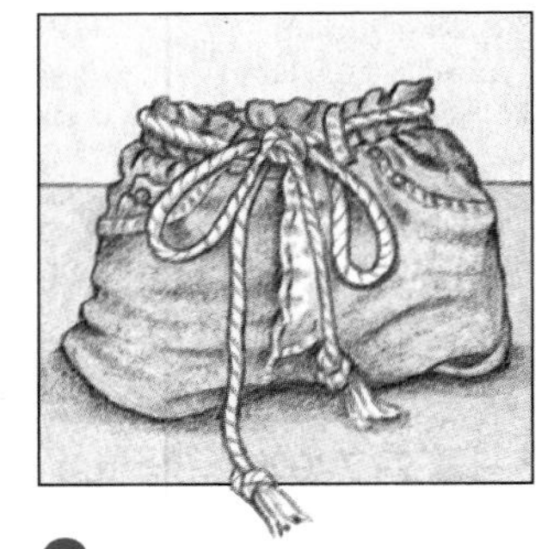

6 **Thread the cord or rope through the belt loops and knot the ends. Pull to close.**

For extra style, try a hand-me-down tie or a splashy sash to close the bag.

Add cute clip-on suspenders for shoulder straps.

Bitty Bag

Turn an old pocket into a mini purse for keys, money, and more—just tuck in a few treasures and you're out the door!

Basic Bag

Cut all the way around the back pocket of an old pair of jeans. Stay as close to the outside edges as you can.

Shoulder Strap

Sew buttons in the top corners. Tie each end of a long ribbon in a double knot around the base of each button.

Button Clasp

Sew a button onto the front layer. Use scissors to carefully poke 2 small holes through both layers behind the button. Thread a piece of ribbon about 12 inches long through the holes. Tie the ends around the button.

Woven Bow

Use a ruler and chalk to make an even number of marks between the left and right seams. With scissors, snip a small slit in the front layer at each mark. Cut 2 ribbons, each 6 inches long. Knot 1 end of each ribbon. Starting inside the pocket, weave 1 ribbon from the left edge to the middle. Weave the other ribbon from the right. Tie a bow where the ends meet.